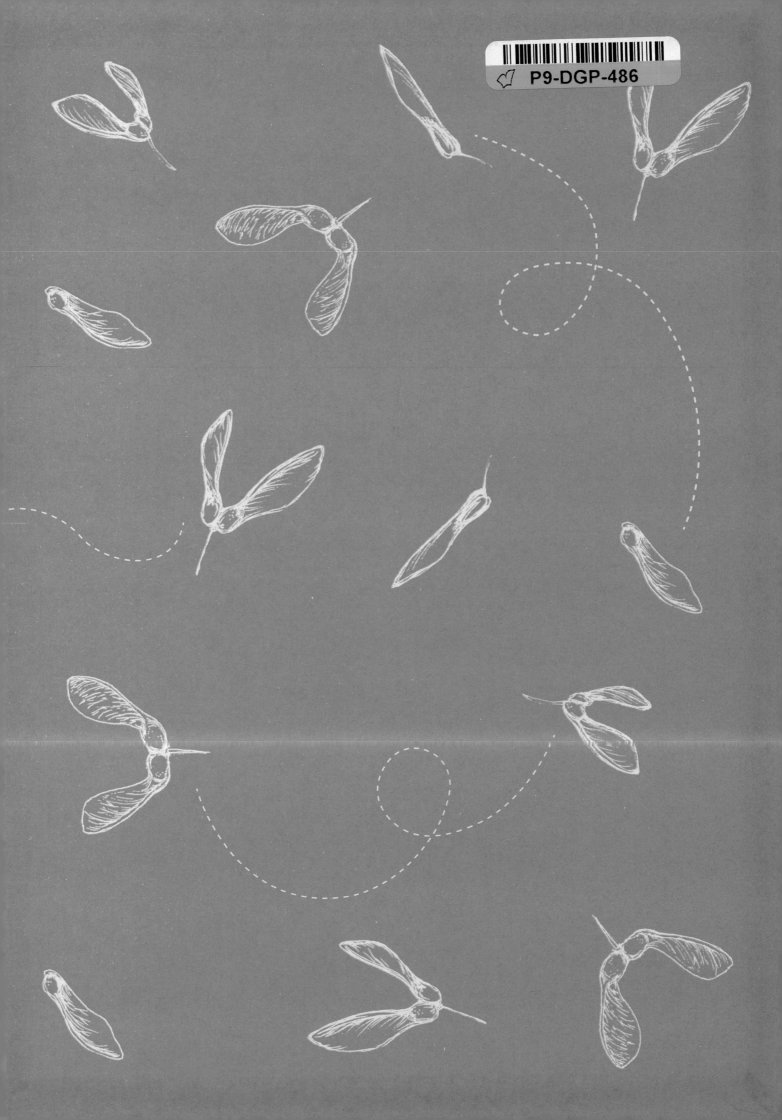

To my mom, Jackie, for helping me grow.
J.W.

For Sam, while you're still a seedling.
L.K.

First published in 2016 by words & pictures
Part of The of Quarto Group
The Old Brewery, 6 Blundell Street, London N7 9BH

This edition published in the United States in 2017
by words & pictures
Part of The of Quarto Group
6 Orchard, Lake Forest, CA 92630

A CIP record for this book is available from the
Library of Congress.

ISBN: 978-1-91027-726-3

Manufactured in Guangdong, China CC102017

3 5 7 9 8 6 4

It Starts With a Seed

Words by Laura Knowles
Pictures by Jennie Webber

words & pictures

It starts with a seed.

But where does it lead?

To a root, to a shoot,
to a few tiny leaves.

As days turn to weeks,
the seedling has grown:
it's a dragonfly perch!
A ladybug throne!

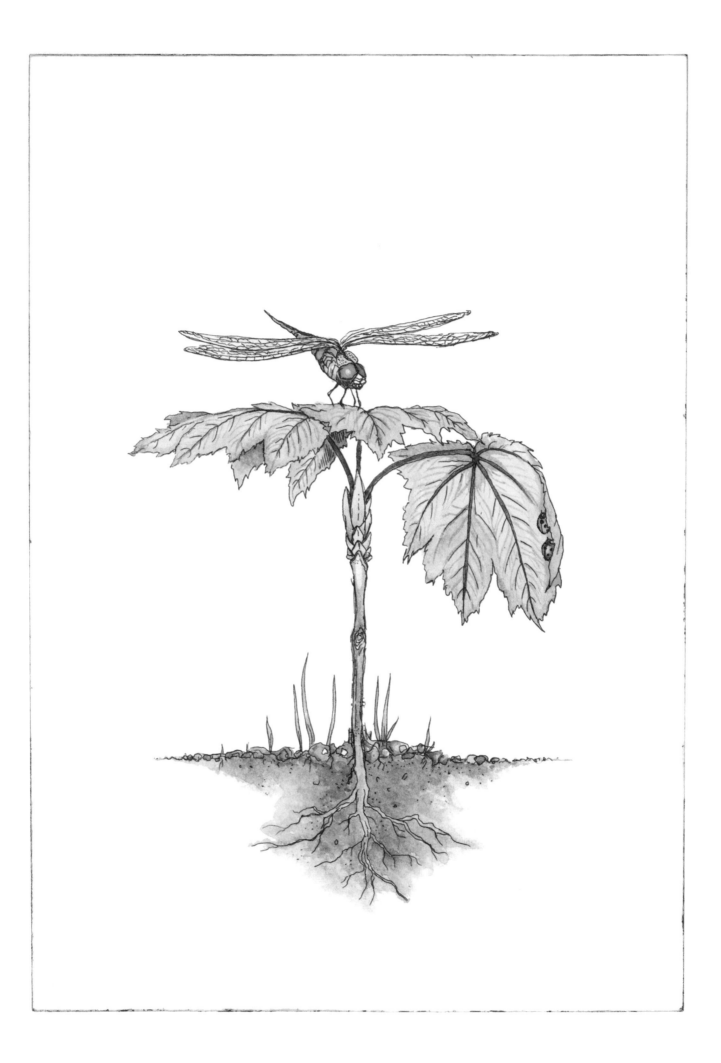

But it wants to grow bigger,
it yearns to climb high.
Pushing down through the dirt,
stretching up to the sky.

How can something so small
turn into a tree,
which is such an incredibly
BIG thing to be?

It takes many seasons;
fall, summer, and spring.
With each passing year
the trunk builds a new ring.

Strong branches reach out,
they give shelter and shade:
a home where the animals
don't feel afraid.

Even in winter,
when the leaves have all dropped,
the tree is asleep,
but life hasn't stopped.

It is waiting for spring,
for the warmth of the sun,
when buds burst from branches.
What color, what fun!

It's not just a tree
but a wonderful world,
full of beetles and grubs
and squirrels and birds.

All busily making
a life of their own,
in their leaf-laden,
bark-bound arboreal home.

The seeds are now ready
to float in the breeze...

...might just grow into...

...new trees.

A sycamore tree can grow 115 feet tall.

A sycamore's sap, pollen, nectar, and seeds attract many insects and birds looking for a tasty meal.

A sycamore tree can live for 400 years.

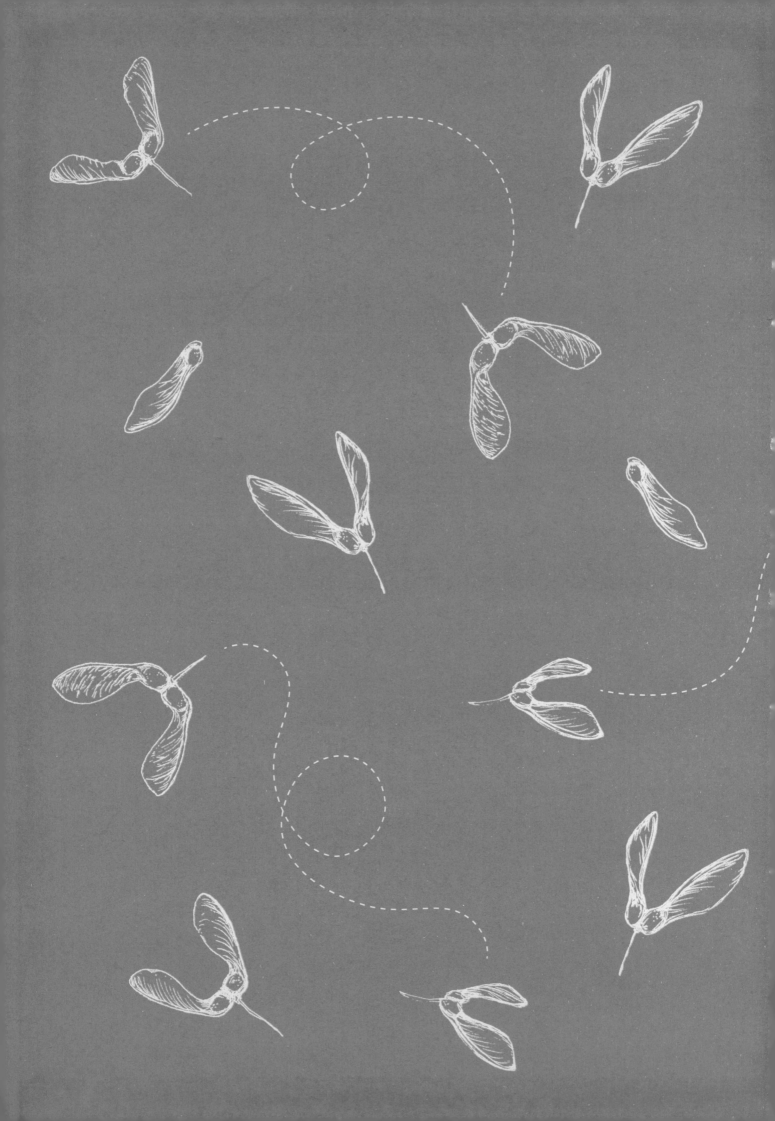